Commu Workbook for Couples

Enhance Conflict Resolution Skills in your Marriage, Build a Strong Relationship and Lasting Love through Dialectical Behavior Therapy

Christian Silverman

LEGAL DISCLAIMER

Table of Contents

Introduction

Congratulations on purchasing *Communication Workbook for Couples,* and thank you for doing so.

With the right tools, couples approach their relationship problems the wrong way. They make many common mistakes: they feed into each other's intense negative emotions, they turn every dispute into a referendum on their relationship, and their arguments cover too many things that can't possibly be resolved in one conversation.

Communication Workbook for Couples uses the foundations of dialectical behavior therapy to get you and your spouse to ask each other the right questions. We tell you ways to think about each question and then give you advice on what to do once you have the answers. The first questions help you figure out how you see yourselves.

After that, our questions get to the heart of your problem, preventing you from losing track of the topic at hand. The last questions will get you through the solutions to your relationship problems, whatever they may be.

Most couples simply don't know how to reach solutions together because they were never given the correct tools. Look at this book as a toolbox to help you with any issues you may run into in your relationship.

Even though married couples often don't know how to resolve their issues when left to their own devices, they find that it isn't nearly as hard as they thought when they have something to work with. This is exactly what the workbook provides you with: something to work with.

Without it, your conversation with your spouse will go in every direction it can. As you may already know from your personal experience, this kind of conversation doesn't land either of you in a place you want to be.

It might be difficult sometimes, but there is no other option than to use the questions given to you here to help sort through the problems in your marriage. They get to the heart of every issue in marriage. That's because all of them are concerned foremost with issues in your communication, from which all problems ultimately stem.

I hope you can come to see them through all of these questions. That theme is to deal with one problem at a time. It is natural for couples to bicker with each other, each feeling justified for defending their side of the story. Everyone thinks they are right.

But no one "wins" if not even a single individual issue is addressed. When you and your spouse keep bickering, even if you are absolutely certain you are right — it doesn't matter that you are right. You won't get anywhere talking to them in this way. It simply isn't productive communication.

Productive communication is the final goal of this book, and of dialectical behavior therapy in general. It means really understanding what your partner is saying, even if you still don't agree. You have to hear what they are saying if you want them to listen to you. When both spouses do nothing more than argue without end, no one accomplishes anything.

By tackling these questions one at a time, you will reach a full understanding of what your spouse believes — not just a caricature of it.

The best strategy is to describe your relationship and compare it to discover where your visions of yourselves as a couple differ. There are sure to be discrepancies between how your partner sees your relationship and how you see it.

Tackle these questions head-on. At some point, you need to come to an agreement on who you are as a couple. You are just going to keep fighting even more if you don't even have the same image of your relationship. This image informs your aspirations and hopes for the future, so it matters deeply.

Once you at least come to a greater agreement on your self-identity as a couple, I want you to take a moment to address all the times you haven't lived up to this image.

It is crucial that you don't make this about individual mistakes. I am not asking you to point out all the shortcomings of your partner. Rather, I want you to notice all the times your idea of who you are as a couple has been challenged. Your concept of yourselves may be pretty accurate, but it can't be perfect. All generalizations have some truth and untruth to them.

Recognizing the imperfection of your expectations is a vital step to resolving relationship problems in general. We all have an idea of what we want from our spouse; our idea of them can become more prominent than reality, however. This is where we run into problems because you have to work with who you have in front of you.

If you create an image of your partner that is somewhat distorted, this is normal. Everyone has some unrealistic ideas of the people around them, and that is fine. But the problem is when you become so attached to that idea that you don't accept reality at all.

You may believe, at first, that the way you personally see yourselves as a couple isn't important. It's easy to think that the more useful approach in therapy would be to prioritize objective perspectives above all else: to note only behaviors and habits, and not subjectivity.

But we still have to pay attention to subjectivity. That's because humans are subjective creatures; when they believe something to be true, it is actually true to them. It matters a great deal if someone believes something to be true, whether they are in touch with reality or not. Belief is a very powerful thing.

Keep that in mind throughout all the questions and exercises in the workbook. You may think that the way your partner sees things is unrealistic or untrue, but that doesn't mean you don't need to respect their ideas and feelings.

Both of your views are emotionally valid, and you should learn to recognize that in each other. It doesn't mean you can't have your own opinions— just remember that how strongly you feel is just as strong as your partner feels.

See their views as they are: coming from a personal place as yours do for you. It will help you get into their mind and understand them.

Give yourselves some space to think about this question on your own. This part of the exercise is important because sometimes we have the truth as we share it with others, but then there is a different truth that we feel when we are alone.

When you have the space to be open with yourself, consider how you really see your relationship. Who do you see yourselves as, even if you wouldn't ever tell your spouse this? Ultimately, you will need to share it with your spouse.

It isn't healthy for your relationship to keep things from each other. You need to feel like you can't be honest about what you think. If you don't feel comfortable sharing with your partner how you feel about your relationship, then you have already found one major cause of issues that needs to be addressed. You may have many other issues to work through, but this is one that absolutely must be confronted.

At the end of the day, couples who do not trust each other enough to speak their mind cannot be healthy and conscious. You should be able to be open about how you view yourselves as a couple. If you can't, this is the first issue you need to tackle. Read on in the workbook to learn how you should tackle it.

There are plenty of books on this subject on the market, thanks again for choosing this one! Every effort was made to ensure it is full of as much useful information as possible. Please enjoy!

Who Are We as a Couple?

This question isn't about how your friends, family, and co-workers see you as a couple. We want you to ask yourselves how you view your relationship. What does no one, even your closest friends, know about your relationship?

In the beginning of courtship, couples believe they are going to last because they feel an emotional closeness with the person that can't be reduced to mere words.

The next question will cut right through to how others do see you as a couple. This is an important question to answer, too, as it will be essential to answering the rest of these questions in dialectical behavior therapy. But for now, I want you to start figuring out how you see yourselves.

Don't think about how others view you. Focus on the thoughts you have inside — the feelings you harbor that may be difficult to put into words.

Most married couples wouldn't say they have a storybook romance. Some do, but many others simply got together because it felt right. You can start answering this question by looking at it from that perspective.

What is your story as a married couple? Are there unique details that keep you together? If so, why?

It is highly likely that the two of you have a story about your romance that you tell other people. You tell it to your family and to your friends. You like to tell this story because, by now, this relationship isn't just about your passion for your spouse. This relationship is part of who you are.

Does your relationship feel like a fairytale romance, or do the two of you have a more real-world approach to your relationship? You might be more realistic or more idealistic. Neither is good or bad; I just want you to know which one you are.

You may have evolved with how you view your relationship. It's likely that you had a more idealistic view of relationships in the beginning than you do now.

Together, have a conversation about this evolution. Do you think your idea of who you are has changed a lot? Did it only change slightly?

You need to be sure to work on your relationship using your new vision of yourselves— not your old one. If you get stuck thinking about your old selves, you'll never get anywhere. It is both unrealistic and unhelpful in resolving your problems. Agree on some version of who you are.

What Type of Relationship Do We Have?

The two of you should now contemplate how others might see your relationship. Don't only think of it as your reputation as a couple — the most important part is to think about how you are seen on the outside.

Answering this question will help you proceed in as objective a fashion as possible. Do people see you as a couple who displays affection publicly? Do they see you fight a lot?

Of course, there is much more to your relationship than what people see from the outside. It is just one more starting point for identifying your main problems.

As you know, however, a successful long-term relationship cannot depend on passion alone. That's why we challenge you to figure out who you are as a couple besides just your emotional closeness.

Perhaps you have already discussed this before as a couple. Think back and figure out if this is the case. The two of you have probably looked at how other couples act before and talked about how you differ from them.

It could be that you don't display as much public affection as they do, or that you display more. Maybe both of you are quieter people compared to your average couple; maybe you are louder. These are some of the things you can start with to figure out what kind of couple you are. Discuss this together for a moment and see if it gets you anywhere.

You might think this is a trivial thing to focus on, but you will find that with all of these questions, subjects that seem shallow at first can easily turn deep. It might not seem ground-breaking to figure out that you and your partner are the kind of couple who have to share everything, or you might be more independent.

They can seem like trivial things to ask yourselves, but knowing who you are as a couple accomplishes a task that helps us work through the upcoming questions.

For one thing, having a sense of identity as a couple gives you a reason to fight for your relationship. It helps you remember all the reasons you are together, despite the times you make each other mad. This is the kind of self-reflection you can do that will seriously help you get to the bottom of the problems in your marriage.

Besides helping you remember who you are as a couple, determining your identity as a couple will help you think of the strengths and weaknesses you have.

The first key lesson of dialectical behavior therapy is that for every strength a couple has, comes a weakness.

You and your spouse may be able to get along like good friends, but this can come with a weakness — you might only be able to talk with each other in a casual, friendly way and not know how to address the serious problems that every couple has to deal with.

On the other hand, you might be two serious people who always work through the tough issues together, but then you never learn how to spend time together companionably.

As you can see, both of these kinds of relationships come with strengths and weaknesses. And it is not the only example of this. For each characteristic you find of your relationship, discuss what strengths and weaknesses come from it with your partner.

A common weakness of relationships is assigning each other specific jobs for the household and not having any cooperation with each other that crosses between these jobs.

For instance, one spouse might be responsible for cooking every day, while the other is responsible for cleaning. It might seem like this is a good way to manage the tasks that need to get done. They do need to get done, after all, and one of you can't do everything. Splitting tasks between the two of you can feel like a good way to manage them.

There is a fundamental problem with having entirely different jobs, though. When the two of you have distinct jobs and don't have any overlap at all, you don't ever learn what the other does. You don't learn how to appreciate what the other does.

It's only one example of what kinds of problems relationships may face, but even if this isn't your specific problem, you can still learn from it. You can get to know the responsibilities of your significant other by picking up some of their tasks every once in a while.

When you do that, it will give you a brand new appreciation for what they do for your household.

It doesn't mean you have to do an equal amount of the work from that responsibility as they do. In fact, splitting tasks between the two of you is still a good idea overall. Otherwise, you will get overwhelmed and not get everything done.

But in an effort to resolve the resentment you may feel of your spouse when it seems like they don't appreciate what you do, you should show them that you appreciate what they do by helping with or completing some of their work for them.

When determining what kind of couple you are, know that there are two dimensions of your identity as a couple: (1) your personality as a couple and (2) your management of practical matters.

The first one was covered in the example of quiet couples versus loud couples and serious couples versus friendly couples. The second one was covered by the example of allocating household tasks.

Spend some time discussing what your identity as a couple is in these two main areas. Once you've done that, you can figure out how you two will handle your issues in a different way from other couples.

Note: you shouldn't try to resolve your problems all right now. This is not what I am asking you to do. I am telling you to figure out how your personality and practicality as a couple will tackle these problems differently from other couples.

What values do the two of you have that might come into play? What models do the two of you have that might have affected the kind of couple you are?

If you don't have questions like this popping into your head already, you should continue reading on through the workbook to get ideas flowing. Asking yourself questions about your identity as a couple is the best way to figure out who you really are.

Don't forget to be thinking about your identity as a couple from an outside perspective. This isn't about how you see yourselves, but how others might see you. It is how you would be described by a third party. It is how a story author might describe you as a couple if you were fictional characters.

A third party would be able to describe how you behave as a couple (your personality) and how you deal with practical matters (your practicality). As an exercise, I would like to ask you and your partner to pretend like you are fiction writers describing the two of you as a couple.

Remember not to describe yourself as individuals; describe you and your partner as one unit. Doing this will help the two of you achieve a more objective view of who you are.

Out of all the questions you and your spouse need to ask each other, this is the one you need to spend the most time on. This is because the workbook can help you with communication skills, emotional skills, and conflict resolution skills — skills that will help you no matter who you are as a couple — but there are still some things that will differ from relationship to relationship.

Every individual is different, and in the same way, every couple is different. The most important lessons of dialectical behavior therapy can be applied to everyone. However, your personality and practicality differences as a couple are still relevant to solving whatever problems you are going through.

Since the workbook can't cover all the ways, different kinds of couples need to solve their problems. You need to spend a significant amount of time figuring out who you are as a couple before you can expect to see any results with your dialectical behavior therapy. Thankfully, this workbook will be with you for the entire process.

After the two of you do the activity pretending you are writers describing who you are as a couple, this should be used to inform the way you tackle the remaining questions in this book. You can resolve any dispute or argument you have if you know who you are.

How Do We Relate With Each Other?

What do you see in each other? What got the two of you together? This is what we mean by how you relate to each other. There is the emotional closeness we mentioned before, which is a staple of every relationship, good and bad.

And then there is the kind of chemistry that comes with only people you love. Throughout the whole workbook, we don't try to understand this element of love like scientists. It can't be understood using the same means we use to improve our communication or behavioral psychology.

However, we can embrace that part of love while trying to get a handle on the more challenging aspects of marriage. The more challenging aspects are not usually the intimate parts, but instead, the practical aspects of relationships are the things that tend to give couples problems.

Studies on couples have shown that practical matters are what cause most serious fights, much more so than anything relating to sexuality or intimacy. That means it behooves you and your partner to use the skills in this book to enable yourselves to talk about your practical day-to-day problems in an effective way.

You need to think beyond how you emotionally support each other and think about the more practical ways you relate. These are the two sides of the relationship coin: the emotional side and the rational side.

The two of you likely relate with each other in an emotional way, because this is how most couples get together. We are mostly past the times of arranged marriages, so when two people are together, it is usually because they actually wanted to form a union — not because they had to.

Ask yourselves why you saw a bond in the first place. You probably had other crushes and romantic engagements before you met each other; there was something different about this particular relationship that led you to take it to the step of marriage.

You may have longed for somebody that was smart, funny, understanding, and experienced, who you could call if something went terribly wrong. When you couple up with your future wife or husband, it is in this period when your relationship forms.

That is the part of relationships that is easy to understand; it is the part of relationships that they always show in the movies and on TV because it isn't as messy and complicated as what happens after you get together.

Next, you have the practical side of the relationship coin. It is probable that you didn't only get together for emotional reasons. You are adults, after all, and we all know that the feelings of excitement from the honeymoon phase fade after some time. That means since you are together, it is probably not completely an emotional thing. You see some practical worth in the other person already.

This will be a great help to you if you can let your partner know what practical benefits they bring to the table. What makes a relationship with them easier in some senses compared to a relationship with someone else?

Think about someone else you may have ended up with instead. It's possible that a person would have given you a much harder time when you came home late from work. You might see more in your spouse when you appreciate these little things they don't do that other spouses would.

Perhaps you think your present spouse has a lot of frustrating habits, but that person would have had some annoying habits, too. They would just have been different ones.

Consider both sides of this coin when you try to answer the question, "How do you relate to each other?" This question deals with a different problem than the last two.

The last two questions were about how you function as a couple practically and how you view your relationship from your individual perspectives. When you think about how you relate to each other, you are thinking about the choices you make every day in the marriage.

There are choices you make automatically, and there are more deliberate choices. You probably don't even realize all the time your spouse puts into the responsibilities they take on in the relationship.

For example, you can make the intentional choice to expect your partner to put in a lot of time at work because you are responsible for the household chores.

Couples tend to overlook this, but such arrangements are what really form a marriage. It is nothing deeper than that: marriage is mostly about the practical, routine arrangements that you have with each other.

It is in both of your best interests that you learn to stop misunderstanding what the other wants. Get to the bottom of what bothers both of you about the current division of responsibilities.

Certainly, this is a hard conversation to have in any relationship. But starting the conversation is much harder than the conversation itself. Both of you have that one thing you are willing to do that the other is not; you pride yourself in it because you feel as if you are contributing to the household.

The problem is that our spouse may tend to take advantage of the things that we do. When they do that, the things we do become invisible to them. They no longer appreciate it at that point.

You may technically know in the back of your mind that they are fulfilling these duties, but that doesn't mean you actually have an understanding of what that means.

When your spouse does that job, that is part of how they relate to you. You might not even think of it that way anymore. Things have been this way for so long that it seems like this is just how things are.

But don't lose sight of how things would be different if you weren't together. All the work your spouse does now would still have to get done if you weren't together, but now you would have to do it on top of everything you already do.

In the same way, think about the work you contribute to the marriage. You might have thought about it as one of your duties in the relationship in the beginning, but it's possible that you forgot about that somewhere along the way, and now you just see it as part of your daily routine.

When your day-to-day life consists of doing things for your household, that means your day-to-day life is filled with relating to your spouse. Don't lose sight of that.

Remember when I told you to isolate the reason why you made the choice to be with your spouse instead of someone else?

The next thing I want you to do is related to this; when you become more aware of all the duties you fulfill every day and the fact that they are ways you relate to your spouse, it is a manner of making these habits a choice rather than mere muscle memory.

It is helpful to have muscle memories that make repetitive tasks easier for us. But the bad thing about them is that we start forgetting the reasons we did them in the first place.

When you become more conscious of how your daily activities are a way of relating to your spouse, you will see them as choices you make every day to stay committed to them.

This will make the work feel more meaningful, and it will make you feel more comfortable about being with them. Your actions will match your feelings and be totally congruent.

It doesn't mean you will never have doubts or frustrations ever again. But when you are more mindful about how your daily life is informed by the commitment you made to your spouse, you will feel better about that work. You will feel like the two of you are doing work together, constantly relating to each other in your daily tasks, even when you are not together physically.

It is a crucial thing to recognize as a married couple because we often get so busy with the everyday things that we don't know why we are doing them anymore.

Get back in touch with all the ways you relate to your spouse with the little choices you make each day, and you will learn how to express more love instead of negativity.

How Do We See Ourselves and Each Other?

Now is the time to make judgments about who the two of you are as individuals. You can rely on your intuition here — there is no need to overthink your identity. You know who you are.

I will ask both of you to keep your own journals, and inside of these journals, you should do nothing but spend some time with yourself and reflect on who you are.

Do this alone; don't stay in the same room as your spouse, even if they aren't looking at what you are writing. It might sound silly, but you will be unconsciously influenced just because your spouse is around.

For the sake of getting your thoughts on paper without any interruptions, you shouldn't think about what your spouse might think while writing in this journal.

You should continue to use this journal throughout the workbook. Keep it private the entire time, but of course, discuss the things you are writing in your communication journal when you feel comfortable sharing it.

You want to create a relationship environment where you both have the right to your own privacy, but you aren't too afraid to share your own thoughts.

Here is one way of looking at it: when you are in a marriage, you have someone who is going to spend more time with you and know you better than anyone else. You can go on with life without sharing your innermost thoughts and feelings, but all of us have these, and they are much harder to deal with when we have to deal with them alone.

Of all people, your spouse should be the person you would be comfortable talking about these things with — if not them, then who?

Now, it's true that you can have confidants outside of your marriage. You should feel totally free to talk about whatever you want with close friends or family members outside of your marriage. A partner who tells you that you can't do this is being overly controlling and creating a toxic, unhealthy relationship.

With all that said, though, you need to have some sort of emotional intimacy with your partner. That should go without saying. You already share the practical parts of your life together. If you share these material things but not the emotional sides of each other, this will only lead to problems, because one person will always end up feeling resentful.

You can avoid this problem by being open about how you see each other and yourselves. Allow yourselves to be vulnerable and really dive into what you may be feeling anxious or upset about.

Share with each other how you view yourselves, and then take turns sharing how you view each other. It doesn't have to be a wholly positive exchange. After all, everyone is a mix of good and bad.

As you would probably guess, this can easily turn into a toxic exchange. It doesn't have to be, but it takes real effort to prevent this from happening. I will give you a few tips to keep the conversation from being an unpleasant or combative one.

First of all, understand the full extent of what the exercise is. Don't do less than the exercise asks of you, but more importantly, don't go further than the exercise intends you to.

The exercise asks you and your spouse to take turns, saying how you view yourselves and how you view each other.

It does not ask you to openly insult each other. It does not ask you to lie about your general view of your spouse, but it doesn't ask you to have a negative or condescending tone, either.

When your partner describes how they view themselves, don't interrupt them with what you think they are getting wrong. The exercise is not to get to "the truth" or to figure out who is right in their evaluations.

Don't forget about the importance of subjectivity in communication. You may really think that someone's beliefs are totally off base, but when it comes down to it, we are talking about your strong beliefs and their strong beliefs.

Whether or not you think your beliefs are more founded in reality does not matter. That goes against the point of communication. Communication must go two ways.

Since we are human beings and human beings tend to be very self-centered, we always put our personal expression over our listening. We assume other people have more to gain from listening to us talk than we have to gain from listening to them.

You are entitled to your view that your partner sees themselves in a distorted way. It may be true, or it may be false. But you have to respect their views on the matter as much as you respect your own.

Both of you know that you are supposed to listen to each other's personal views, so if you listen to them self-reflect without interrupting, they will be more likely to do the same for you. When that happens, you will feel much better about opening up to them. You will feel more free to speak your mind in the future.

With all of dialectical behavior therapy, this is the goal: you want to learn how to be comfortable hearing ideas you don't agree with, and not pounce in with a rebuttal right away. Learn to simply let dissenting ideas exist, and be comfortable with the fact that people around you do not always have the same ideas as you. That extends to your spouse.

As long as you go into the activity in good faith, you should be able to say what you think of each other without fear of repercussions.

What Do I Bring to the Relationship?

When we asked how you related to each other, this was asking why you are together in the first place. This question covers the more pragmatic issues in a marriage: namely, what does each of you contribute to the household?

It is so easy to focus on what our spouse can do more of. We want them to pick up more of the work we are doing because we feel it is harder than what they may be doing.

But I challenge you to only focus on what you bring to the relationship. For this question, don't think at all about what your partner could do more of. Couples who answer this question honestly realize what they could be doing better, and they get better at recognizing times when they should be helping their spouse more.

But this can only be possible if you start with yourself and how you could do better. If you focus on your spouse; instead, they will become naturally defensive, you will become frustrated that they don't agree with what you are saying, and nothing will be accomplished.

With the focus on yourself, you do not have to feel insecure about your marriage. It only takes one person to bring your marriage into disarray — and then you will be left picking up the pieces.

Instead, learn how to be an example for your spouse to follow. You can't expect them to be better if you aren't changing your behavior.

If you personally think your spouse could do a better job of helping clean the dishes instead of expecting you to do them every night, pick up one of the household duties they usually do.

Don't say anything explicitly about it. If you do that, you will be setting up expectations, and that will not get you the results you want. All you want to do is show your spouse you appreciate what they do by taking on some of their workload. They will see how thoughtful you are being and feel inspired to return the favor.

There are countless ways a spouse can do their fair share for the relationship and for their livelihood, so we aren't only talking about keeping house or making money. This includes everything in marriage as a whole: doing taxes, picking up children from school and activities, keeping up with other families, planning for holidays, and the list goes on.

One of the major hurdles that couples run into when they try this is a simple knowledge gap. It makes sense that married couples would run into this problem. If your spouse is always responsible for doing taxes every year, you simply expect them to do it.

The first time they ask you to do it, you don't even know where to start. You have no knowledge to go off of because you relied on them to do the taxes.

This is where cooperation and patient teaching will come in handy. The spouse who knows how to do something will have to show their other half how things are done.

When you are the teacher, do your best to show your spouse how to do things in a respectful and patient way. It can be very easy to get mad at our partner for not picking it up quickly enough, especially when it feels like they always just expected us to do it.

But if they were willing to try to do some of it for you, be open to that and keep a positive attitude while you teach them, even if you get frustrated.

Times are changing, but women still run into the issue of being expected to do the unpaid work that comes with having children, including doing housework, arranging school activities, signing papers, having summer plans, and so forth. It can be an exhausting expectation for mothers whether or not they also work regular jobs.

If you think you have this problem, start a dialogue with your spouse about the stress it puts on you. The key to doing this successfully is making it clear that you aren't asking them to suddenly take on all these tasks for you at the same time. All you want is some help.

With any of these tasks that come with having a larger household, you can find the common theme of having stakes. Here is what I mean by this: you might know on the surface that your spouse does task X, but it doesn't mean you know all the little things task X actually entails.

When you barely understand what this task means, it leads you to think of it as simple. When you don't understand something, the placeholder you have for it is much less complicated than the real thing.

You have no concept of how long it takes, and you have no concept of the mental labor that accompanies it.

That's why it will help your relationship tremendously if the two of you force yourselves to take an interest in learning all the tasks that the other normally does. The only way you can make this happen is by doing them — or at least taking part in some way.

Even if you only do a menial task that is part of the larger task, you will gain more appreciation for what your spouse does than you had before. You can go back to the responsibilities you had before, but you will go back wiser about the things your spouse does.

We can't help that when we have no knowledge about something, we tend to see it as much easier or simpler than it really is. The most common dispute for all couples is the distribution of household work.

It is such a persistent issue because each spouse believes their significant other does not truly understand how much work they do, while at the same time, they don't really understand what their partner does, either.

The solution to this common problem is simple. Do just a little bit of what your spouse does, and you will have more respect for what they add to the relationship.

What Are My Personal Goals?

There is who you are as a person, and then there are your goals.

It isn't human nature to be happy with what we have and where we are in life. Sometimes, this is to our detriment. Especially these days, people could stand to be happy with where they are instead of always hoping for more. When you do nothing but aim for more, you're never happy. You're never satisfied with what you have.

At the same time, goals are a good thing to have. Without them, we feel directionless or hopeless. They give you something to live for. I just talked about the other extreme, but if you were always just happy with things as they were, that wouldn't be good for you either. It is good for your personal development to always have more to strive for.

An upcoming question will help you figure out your goals as a couple, but here we just want you to think about yourself. Start with short-term goals and work your way up to long-term goals.

You might need some help thinking through these. It would be all right to talk to your spouse about what they believe your personal goals are. If you have been vulnerable with them about your dreams before, they may already have a solid idea of what you want to do with your life in the future. Just ask them what they think your goals are; it can put you on the right track to figuring them out.

Don't rely on your spouse exclusively for this, though. It is fine if they help you get started, but I would like to challenge you to spend some time with your communication journal brainstorming ideas for your future plans.

You shouldn't be afraid to write about what you want out of life in that journal. It is only for you. No one is grading it, and if you keep it somewhere private, you don't need to be concerned about anyone reading it either.

Your spouse and your journal are not your only options for thinking of goals. You should also ask other close people in your life about what your goals should be. It can be a little embarrassing to talk about our goals with others, but it is an important thing to know, so we stay in relationships that make us feel supported.

The only one who can answer this question is you. If you're unsure how to answer it, know that there are many people out there in the same position. Don't force an answer upon yourself that you don't believe in.

Maybe it will lead to success, or maybe you'll feel guilty about taking that risk. Whatever the case, do what makes you happy. It's better to know than to not know, and sometimes you just have to try. If you can't agree on anything, ask yourself if you can find common ground. The key is to communicate and not just argue.

You might not think this will help you, but I still want you to try it. After going through things with your spouse, loved ones, and your journal about your personal goals, I want you to meditate on it.

That's right— don't try to put it into words. All you need to do is tell yourself briefly that you are wondering what your goals are. After that, don't intentionally think about anything. Let your thoughts land where they fall.

If you have not spent much time meditating before, as is the case with many people, you may be tempted not to try this exercise at all. Many people are scared to spend any amount of time alone in silence.

While I want you to try it, I don't want to give you the wrong impression of the exercise, either. I am not asking you to spend thirty or even fifteen minutes by yourself thinking about your goals. I only ask that you try to do nothing but contemplate this for ten minutes.

You might not come up with any ideas within ten minutes, and that is okay. The main point of the exercise is not to get immediate results, although that could happen. The point is to get your mind going on the topic.

As you may be aware, your brain is filled with both conscious and unconscious networks. A lot of your brain is simply unavailable to your conscious mind. This is the part of your brain where your dreams originate. It reveals to us what we truly desire and what scares us.

Doing this exercise is similar to thinking about the topic you want to dream about for the explicit purpose of dreaming about it. By dedicating a short amount of time to do nothing but ponder your goals, you are forcing your brain to think about it. You don't leave your brain the opportunity or space to think about anything else that can distract it.

You probably won't have a eureka moment during the short period of time you set aside to focus on your goals, but you are activating all the right buttons, all but guaranteeing your brain will come to some answer later on.

You may not be able to answer it right away. Take some time to calmly reflect on it. As long as you don't put any pressure on yourself, this will lead you to an answer.

This only gets you to the flat answer of your short-term and long-term goals, however. There are a couple of other important matters at hand, though. Namely, you have to determine your means of chasing these dreams, and you have to determine how your relationship fits into these goals.

Of course, figuring out how you will take the actual steps towards achieving your goals can be even harder than the goals themselves. I can't tell you any simple tricks for doing it, but I can say this: doing small things every day that help advance your goal will get you there much better than any one grand action. Incorporate your goals into your daily life, and you will have a much easier time of achieving them.

Finally, have an honest conversation with yourself about how your spouse fits into these goals. There are a number of reasons why your spouse might impede your goals, but there are a number of reasons they may help you with them, too.

The best possible situation is having a spouse who emotionally supports you in your personal goals, helps you take practical steps to achieve them, and doesn't do anything intentional or otherwise to discourage you from achieving them.

Usually, unconsciously, we tend to already be with people who help us succeed in our goals. There is a very good chance your spouse already does this, so it is your job to start being more gracious for that. Not everyone has this privilege, so be happy that you do.

Would I Rather Be Right or Be Loved?

In the moment of a heated disagreement, couples get tunnel vision and care about only one thing: winning the argument. Human beings are built for living in the present moment, so it makes sense that we tend to let it take precedent over everything else.

However, in a stable, healthy, and conscious relationship, we need to learn and practice conflict resolution skills. This truth is the DNA of this entire book.

In order to let go of our compulsion to win the argument, both partners have to take a break from talking for a while and think about what it is you are actually arguing about. Since these fights have a tendency to go wildly in many different directions, this is much easier said than done.

Both of you want to focus on the thing that matters most — and to complicate matters even further, each of you have a long list of frustrations that you want to throw at your significant other.

Couples approach conversations with their significant other as though they are going onto a battlefield instead of as a conversation. This is far from the ideal for a productive conversation that meets the standards of dialectical behavior therapy.

When you go into a conversation expecting an adversary rather than a companion, you put your defenses up. You aren't ready to be open with your spouse. You're only ready to defend your ideas against their attacks.

You're not ready to know about your spouse's deepest weaknesses. You're not ready to admit to yourself that maybe you're not the one who can make the best of a bad situation.

And, most importantly, you're not ready to admit that you are sometimes a little sad, sometimes a little hopeless, sometimes a little scared, or maybe sometimes a little less confident.

Be open to whatever you will learn along the way because you are sure to be surprised at some juncture.

To avoid having tunnel vision like this, give yourself some space to ask yourself what you want out of communication with your spouse before the communication even begins.

In other words, plan out how productive communication would go with your spouse before you actually see them and try to make it happen.

When you plan something mentally before you do it, there are many benefits. You won't feel as nervous about speaking what is on your mind, for one. It's never good to hold back what you think because of fear of how others will react. You should always feel free to speak your mind and nothing less with your partner.

Another benefit is being prepared for anything negative that might happen during the exchange. Now, remember that your spouse probably doesn't mean anything of it if they sometimes unintentionally upset you when you open up to them.

But even at a time, you might normally get your feelings hurt; you won't anymore when you mentally prepare yourself first. You have considered and know the kinds of things that might happen before you try it.

Mental preparation is just one of many conflict resolution skills that will enable you to have more productive conversations with your spouse. Of all the different conflict resolution methods, mental preparation is considered proactive because it is meant to prevent conflict from even happening instead of dealing with it after it does happen.

There are other methods of conflict resolution, as well. You will find them worthwhile if you are trying to make a conversation work instead of getting frustrated with your partner and just giving up on communication with them.

You can fight, get angry, or attempt to divert, distract, or compromise with your partner. You can block people out and talk to people in another way. You can say no without giving a reason and teach your partner you don't give any reason.

Everyone thinks they are right. There is no getting around it. But with good conflict resolution skills stemming from dialectical behavioral therapy, you can look at communication as an area you can improve upon instead of as a constant source of frustration.

One such conflict resolution skill involves something called "I" statements. Any couple who has been through traditional therapy before should be familiar with this term.

On the surface, you may think an "I" statement is simply a sentence that starts with "I." This can be a sign of an "I" statement; however, the mere fact that a sentence starts with this word doesn't tell you that you are looking at an "I" statement.

More specifically, an "I" statement is a sentence where you express how you react to things and what you do. You don't use an "I" statement to put the blame on someone else or try to paint a picture of someone as the bad guy.

I told you that "I" statements aren't just sentences starting with "I" because it is a common problem for couples to learn about "I" statements without this definition, and then not improve in their communication at all. It's because they continue to blame their spouse for everything and portray them in the worst possible light, but they will do it with sentences starting with "I":

I feel so upset when you don't pick up your clothes.

This sentence may start with an "I," but it's not an "I" statement. It is an emotional accusation. A true "I" statement would put the focus on what makes the speaker feel good instead of telling a story about how their spouse makes them upset:

I feel happy when the room is tidy.

Know the difference between these two sentences and deeply understand why the second one better conveys the speaker's idea. Even if you only start more sentences with "I" instead of "You," you will still notice your communication is improving, if only because you don't sound as accusatory.

However, learning to employ real "I" statements like the second sentence will make you one of the best communicators, you know. It all comes down to being positive and affirmative instead of negative and accusatory.

Effective use of "I" statements will make a notable difference in the amount of productive communication you have with your spouse. As long as you make your goal to be patient and loving with them instead of just to win the fight, you have a great chance of having productive conversations.

Can I Trust You?

There are many ideas out there about what makes a relationship work. Some say passion; some say commitment. As you go through these questions and give your spouse the honest truth, it should become apparent that what makes a marriage work is the same thing that makes any relationship work: trust.

Of course, trust and commitment have much in common. The first exercise I want you and your partner to do is define trust together. Ask yourselves what trust means for you, and what it means for your relationship.

After doing this exercise, it should be easier to figure out what the difference between commitment and trust is. As defined in dialectical behavior therapy, commitment is the action we take to stay with our spouse through thick and thin. Trust is the reason we commit to them — whether those reasons are emotional, practical, or from our experiences with them.

The big difference between a marriage and a relationship is that you need to be there for each other in almost every aspect of your lives. That's why the strength of your trust must be much greater than for any other relationship. Even the smallest hint of doubt in your trust for your spouse has remarkable consequences.

Commitment is less of a problem when you falter on it from time to time. All of us are human, so sometimes we do not act as though we are as committed to the relationship as we should be. This is normal, and it does not mean we are not taking the relationship seriously.

Falling below a certain threshold with our trust in our spouse is a different story. We don't have the option to place little trust in them, because we are relying on them.

When we feel we can't rely on the one person we should be able to rely on, it leads to some real problems. A relationship where one partner doesn't trust the other, or where neither partner trusts the other, will not last.

There is a physical component to trust, too. Although the bulk of this book concerns itself with the emotional and psychological dimensions of relationships, the sexual, sensual, and romantic dimensions are not something you can ignore.

It depends on your specific relationship, too. You might be the kind of couple that falls back on sexual trust to reaffirm your trust in other areas of life. Alternatively, you might treat it as an entirely separate issue.

Both ways are valid, and this is why I had you objectively determine what kind of couple you were at the beginning of the workbook.

Trust doesn't have to be static. It is something that can come and go. You might think you trust someone at first, but then you learn more about them, and you don't trust them anymore.

It is the same way in relationships. Maybe you want to trust your spouse — or you want them to trust you — but something happens that led to your trust in each other diminishing. There are actionable steps you can take to make your trust in each other go back up.

The first is to make your words meaningful. Part of this is telling the truth and not lying. When you find out your partner lies a lot, it becomes incredibly challenging to think anything they say means anything. You start to question everything they say, even if they aren't lying anymore.

This problem will eventually occur in every relationship. If your partner has been lying to you, why would you believe anything they say to you? The truth is, they have lied before. After having been in an abusive relationship for a while, your subconscious brain has a lot of emotional and logical problems when it comes to handling being lied to.

If your partner has never lied to you before, it is most likely a sign that they are a great person and are highly capable of being a good father.

If you used to lie and want to recover your relationship from that phase, you need to affirmatively tell your partner that you are dedicated to not lying anymore. Tell them that from this point on, you only say what you mean. Anything you say, you mean.

I have talked a little bit about vulnerability throughout the book. Vulnerability is a huge component of trust.

It is basically the same in all relationships — not just romantic ones. People feel more willing to trust you when they feel like you are opening yourself up to them — when you are being vulnerable.

You may wonder why this would be the case. It's because when we trust someone to do something for us, we need to place some faith in them. It puts us in a vulnerable position ourselves when we trust someone because if they betray us, they could hurt us.

Therefore, when someone allows us to see their vulnerability, it makes us feel better in turn about being vulnerable with them. We become more willing to share our secrets with them and trust them.

With your spouse, try to open up about the things that bother you. Share your insecurities with them. By doing this, you will make them feel like they can trust you because you are being vulnerable with them.

There is another important way for you to regain trust from your partner: you have to give them the benefit of the doubt.

This is a theme that you may have noticed come up again and again in this workbook. You have to allow people to be better in order to let them improve. Constantly criticizing your partner for their past mistakes is justified on some level. However, if you want them to ever change, you need to keep these criticisms to yourself.

People become what we tell them they are. Telling your spouse that they are lazy will lead them to start seeing themselves as lazy.

Then, they will start doing things that lazy people do. You will believe they were just lazy all along, and that your labeling them had nothing to do with it.

Trust isn't the same for everyone. There are personality types who are more trusting of others, while other personality types have issues trusting a single person. Even when we trust one person over everyone else, you still might not trust them completely.

I am not telling you and your spouse to put aside all doubts about your partner. What I am saying is that you will both make mistakes. Some of them very big.

Even when this happens, though, you have to keep on trusting your spouse. The trust you have in them should not come from the fact that they are perfect every day, but from that, your spouse tries to be better every day. When they are demonstrating to you that they want to be better for you, you should be open to trusting them.

Do We Both Feel We Can Speak Openly?

When both halves of a couple answer this one honestly, it reveals the status of your trust. How comfortable are you saying what you genuinely think to your partner? This is the most objective measure there is of your trust in your partner. If one partner can't even say what they really think, there is no trust.

You won't be able to communicate with each other to any meaningful degree as long as this is true, so it is a problem that must be nipped in the bud right away.

Sometimes people don't know what to do now that they have the information because they are afraid if they say or do anything, they will be cast as crazy.

Are you able to really open up in conversations with your partner? Open and honest communication in a relationship can be especially hard when you're trying to discuss a difficult issue. How often have you walked away from a conversation with your partner feeling angry, disappointed, or misunderstood?

How often have you said things you regretted, things that hurt your partner unnecessarily? In the heat of the moment, we tend to forget how to be kind, patient, and loving. Here are some suggestions to help you really open up communication in your relationship.

Important conversations shouldn't be put off, but neither should they be initiated at awkward or inappropriate times. Don't bring up your bedroom issues at the beginning of the Super Bowl or launch into a serious talk on your way to a holiday party. Make a plan to speak if you have to.

Set aside a specific time so that neither of you is taken aback by the discussion. And never start a conversation when you're too angry to see your partner as anyone other than a terrible devil-person. Wait until you've calmed down a bit.

Conversations—especially the deep ones—rarely go smoothly and hardly ever go as planned. They twist and turn, a tangent here, an unexpected comment there. Don't be rigid when you're talking with your partner.

The more attached you are to how you want the conversation to play out, the more disappointed you'll be by how it does.

Move with the dialogue, bend with it — be in the moment with what's happening between the two of you. You can still share what you need to share, but you may end up having to do it differently than you planned. And that's OK.

Why Do We Disagree?

This is the point where you should come together and agree on one thing: what exactly are you fighting about? It is surprising how often couples get so bent out of shape from the bickering that they can't easily articulate what they are upset about.

Even if you have never engaged in an explicit fight, realize that you most likely have in some capacity. If you find yourself in the middle of a fight, one of the best ways to go about diffusing the tension is to immediately recognize and name the underlying issues.

However, if there are issues, you feel very strongly about, or beliefs you like and want to keep, or two points on which you do not agree, then you need to practice effective conflict resolution skills.

The only way to get to the bottom of this question is for each of you to first answer this question on your own, and then respectfully explain to your spouse what you think you disagree on.

Remember that you can't tackle every problem at once, so even if you are upset about a great number of things, you need to go through just one at a time. Otherwise, the conversation will simply devolve into an argument as it did before.

I will ask each of you to spend some time with your journals to write about what you think the problem is. Remember not to think too deeply when answering the question. Answer the question above and nothing more: what do the two of you disagree about? Don't try to diagnose the "key issue" with your relationship right now.

It is very tempting to do this. Especially when we are thinking deeply about our relationship with our spouse, it sets us on all kinds of trains of thought that make us feel like psychologists.

Don't try to be a psychologist. This is something that we are trying to do with each of these questions: we want to keep on track. It is so easy to get lost by trying to diagnose our marriage as armchair psychiatrists.

Think small. Don't say: I think the problem is that we don't listen to each other enough. Instead, say, "I don't feel listened to when I try to tell my spouse what is stressing me out at work."

Notice the huge difference between these two things. The first one is you are trying to be an armchair psychiatrist. You are trying to find the "root issue" by taking on this role.

But that isn't what is going to solve your issues with your spouse. It will actually lead to more problems because you will tell them what you think about their character as a whole instead of staying focused on the specific situation you are in.

When you think about it, that is obviously just going to make your spouse mad. We don't want that. We don't want to solve big, "root" problems. We want to resolve specific disagreements, one at a time.

This is the key to the success of dialectical behavioral therapy: that we force ourselves to focus on specific situations one at a time instead of losing track of what we even started arguing about, to begin with.

It's important to note that self-regulation is a combination of knowing what you're capable of in a given situation, being willing to control that behavior, and then dealing with those limitations when they present themselves.

We all need some self-regulation. Nobody goes around making apologies and bowing out of every argument. Some people put up with arguments because they're good at them. Others aren't.

The good news is that we don't need to control all of our behavior; oftentimes, that's the very thing we're resisting.

Also, don't overthink your answer to this more limited question. When you are writing in your journal about what your disagreement is, simply let your thoughts flow. You will just get yourself tangled in a mess of thoughts if you don't simply let your thoughts flow.

Allow your hand to do the work of putting your thoughts to words with the pen, instead of getting bogged down by getting your ideas into precise words.

Any time you notice you are stopping yourself from writing something down, ponder why that is. Why would you stop yourself from jotting down the thought?

If you are serious about resolving the dispute with your partner, you shouldn't want to lie to yourself. That won't help you in any way; it will only hurt you.

You are sure to spend a little bit of time looking at space while trying to come up with what to write in your journal, and that's okay. I have two goals you should set for yourself when you are getting this entry down.

The first one is to keep asking yourself if you think your journal entry is done. Once you confidently feel like you are not leaving anything out, you can move on to the next phase of this activity. It is just a feeling you will get that you are done. Don't overanalyze this feeling; simply believe it.

Your second goal is to keep moving your pen. It can be a difficult thing to do, but I don't want you to spend any time in your head thinking about what to write. Of course, this is just a goal. You won't be perfect.

But as long as you make an effort to limit the gaps between writing your words down and thinking about what they will be, you will get closer to approaching your unique perspective on the situation with your spouse.

Next, once both of you have your perspectives about the disagreement on paper, you can come together and figure out what matches in your stories and what does not. You don't have to read exactly what you have written to each other, but you should try to be open with each other. Respectfully share what you wrote down; only discuss your entry.

If you go outside of your entry, you will end up back where you started, talking over each other instead of communicating productively. This is why you should also take turns sharing what you wrote in your entries. If it is necessary, you may toss a coin to determine who will talk first.

Do not interrupt your spouse while they tell you their version of things. There is only one thing you can correct them on, and you should only do it respectfully and after they have shared their side of the story. That is, ask for clarification if they're too broad.

You are allowed to correct each other for this one because it is that important to the success of this activity. It is extremely important that you only try to come to a shared conclusion about what the two of you are disagreeing about, and nothing more.

Surely, there are many disagreements that you could choose from, but the trick here, and everywhere else in the workbook, is trusting that you will address all of them when you need to. Trying to tackle them all at one is not going to resolve anything, so be patient and deal with them as they come.

What Are the Biggest Disagreements We Have?

After you identify what exactly you have recently fought about, you need to agree on something else: what your most significant disagreement is about. This will be an issue that comes up again and again and doesn't seem to go away.

It comes up in the morning, and it comes up at night. It is the disagreement that you are the most likely to have in public because it is so emotionally charged that you can't control yourself on the issue.

You already trained yourselves to focus on one disagreement at a time with the last exercise. This will be tremendously helpful when you try to get to the heart of what your most common disagreements are about.

As usual, you need to be careful not to try to psychoanalyze yourselves and each other. Your only goal is to go through what disagreements you have and determine which ones are the most common ones.

These should not be too hard to identify. They will be the first disagreements that pop into your mind; write these down in your journals individually and then come together to see if you agree.

It's hard to talk through things rationally because you're emotionally invested in the debate. But you have to remember that your spouse cares, too. Your own feelings are not the only ones you should account for.

No one likes to fight. Both of you wished that you never fought or argued. It is easier to make promises that you will keep your emotions under control than it is to actually control them. Throughout the workbook, you will find countless methods to make this happen.

The first piece of advice I have for you to achieve this goal is the following: it is not always about you. Always prioritizing your own feelings over your partner's is not how you will get to some resolution with them. If you make a habit of considering their feelings more, you will learn to be more empathetic.

You will realize how much your own strong negative emotions stem from wanting to defend yourself instead of watching out for your spouse's feelings.

It will be vital for you to work on this skill so you can properly answer this question: what are your biggest disagreements?

Answering this question can potentially tread into some dangerous territory because you are less focused on one topic. As you know, the key to dialectical behavior therapy is staying focused on one issue at a time.

But inevitably, you will have to broaden slightly so you can confront the core problems. Please do not take this as permission to devolve into chaotic arguments with your spouse that do not lead anywhere fruitful.

All of this is only to say, the broader the subject of conversation becomes, the easier it is to go off the rails into a non-productive conversation. Even with a broader topic like this question, the key is to focus on answering this specific question and nothing else.

One of the saddest feelings in life is to know that a person feels unloved or undervalued. We don't want to feel that way about ourselves. All it takes is for someone to offer support for us to open up to others. But it's hard to know when it's going to happen, and you have to take the lead. You have to take the lead in loving yourself first.

Whether that's because you can't have what you want or you're afraid of getting hurt, you can't control anyone else's choices. But you can control your own reactions, and recognizing that it's always on you to control them.

There will inevitably be emotions that get in the way of a productive discussion, and you should expect this. But you can both still make an effort to push emotions aside as much as you can. The trick to it is having the shared goal of figuring out what your main disagreements are.

Imagine that you are therapists looking at your relationship from the outside, except you were able to watch the two of you in all your private conversations and all the things you said.

Looking at it from this perspective will help you problem-solve instead of getting wrapped up in your emotions and petty arguments. You are better off trying to examine your relationship issues from as objective a point of view as you can.

Now, any time I tell you to be objective, I am not issuing a gag order preventing you from ever voicing your emotions. When your emotions naturally come up, you should talk about them as long as you are respectful.

Be the one to offer to listen to your spouse before you talk. When you make this offer, actually listen to the words they say when they are talking. The response you will get from doing that will be overwhelmingly positive; human beings are always worried about not being listened to. Validating them by making a point to listen will do wonders for your relationship.

As you may have already figured out, there is more to this question than what is being directly asked. Yes, I want the two of you to come to a shared conclusion about what your main disagreements are. But that is only half of the challenge here.

The other half is learning how to have serious conversations together. It will require getting better at diving into hard topics without going off the rails.

Now, that is a very hard thing to do. Both of you may fall short of your goals constantly. But you have to do it for a while longer until you notice any improvements.

Do not give up on each other just because you don't want to feel bad for failing. Own up to your own failures, and your spouse will live up to theirs. You do have to trust them to own up to their mistakes as well; if you lead by example, they will feel free to do it, too.

A supportive couple does not always have to agree. But they are supportive of each other's positions. They understand the inherent subjectivity of human ideas. Therefore, they are OK with the fact that they and their spouse do not always agree.

The activity that falls under this question is the hardest one you have had so far, but if you apply all the skills you have learned so far, you will be able to do it. Be forgiving of each other's shortcomings; be ready to fail yourself, but still move on from it every time you do.

Now, back to the matter of answering the actual question itself. Hopefully, the two of you follow the advice provided in this chapter so you can get some idea of what your most common disagreements are. After you have a good conversation about it and have some ideas, there is something new I need you to do.

You both have your own communication journals you have been writing in. I don't want you to use a third journal, if possible, use a chalkboard, whiteboard, or something similar, although you can if you don't have anything else available.

Ideally, you have a relatively large surface that you can write on together. Of course, you will want to be sure it stays in a place where no one besides the two of you will see it, so you feel free to write whatever you want on it.

After you have this whiteboard or whatever large surface you choose to write on, make a list of the big disagreements you came to in your dialogue.

Really take a few moments to read the list you have put together on the whiteboard. Ask yourselves if there are any you can eliminate.

I don't want you to take out any on the list that you think is important. Don't ever do that. However, try your best to eliminate any disagreements you listed that you think can wait until later.

That's because, as I keep emphasizing, focus is key with dialectical behavior therapy. You can always come back to the disagreements you remove later. You won't forget them, because if they are so important, they will come up again. But having a short enough list on this whiteboard will be integral to working through your problems together.

Try to aim to keep three disagreements on this board at maximum. There is a chance that you will not even have to eliminate anything, because you have already narrowed things down enough in your conversation. But if not, it is the last thing you must do before continuing to the next question.

Where Did the Hurdles in Our Relationship Begin?

It may be hard to determine the exact time your rough patch started, or it may be the easiest thing in the world.

But one thing is sure to happen: your spouse will have one idea about where your problems started, and you will have a completely different one. Your answers may not even be similar.

It is an incredibly frustrating thing to happen; when your spouse thinks you both started fighting for a totally different reason, it makes you feel like you'll never be able to resolve your problems. But try to notice how this is your armchair psychiatrist is coming out: you believe that it matters a lot because you won't get to the "root" of your problems until you come to an agreement on this.

It is no different from anything else we have gone over so far. You may think your view of what caused the disagreements is the only one that can be true, but you have to remember that your spouse feels just as strongly. To them, it seems totally crazy that you wouldn't see things the way they do. You may think it's totally different, but it isn't.

This question is much different from the previous one because while you had to come to a shared understanding of your common disagreements in the last question, that is not the case with this question.

Inevitably, you will both have distinct ideas of the main cause of the disagreements were. It simply isn't reasonable to expect the two of you to come to a shared understanding with this one. It is a much deeper question than the last. When you figure out what your common disagreements are, at least you can point out specific, recent examples to find your answer.

But with this question, you are articulating the story of what started it all. It isn't as easy as making a list. You are each making a cause-and-effect relationship between things that happened in your lives and the hurdles you are experiencing now.

You may think at first that it's an easy question because, with a "when" question, it seems like we are just pointing out a day on the calendar. But you two have to do a lot more than that to answer the question because to find a "day on the calendar" that your relationship started having problems, you need to have some reasoning behind why you think it is this day. The previous question was a little broader than the one before it, and this one is the broadest yet.

Even as these questions get broader, you will have to learn how to keep the discussions as narrow as you can to succeed in productive conversation.

That might seem impossible to do with a question as broad as "When did our problems begin?" But learning how to keep the conversations focused and narrow is only a matter of scale. Let me give you an example.

Sure, it's hard to stay on topic with a question that you have to justify by asking what might be the broadest question of all: why are we fighting? But it can get much broader than that, and when it does, that is when things start to get too chaotic.

You might tell your spouse you think your problems started in the wintertime when budgeting started becoming an issue. Notice how this is the broadest you have come so far through any of these questions, but it sticks to the question and doesn't venture beyond it.

There is certainly potential for flying right past the question and entering territory that is hazardous to a productive conversation. You could have said, "I think our problems started when you got cranky that you lost your job in the wintertime."

You might think the last one in your head, but it's easy to see why your spouse wouldn't want to listen to you. For one thing, you used a clear you-statement instead of a true "I" statement. That will surely get your spouse to resent you.

But that's not all. The bigger problem with this wording is it goes beyond the bounds of answering the question objectively.

The first, better version, doesn't hide the truth. It still faces the fact that the two of you had financial stresses in winter. But it faces this fact without simultaneously putting the blame on your spouse, and basically saying they are the root problem.

Even when you mean well, you will find how easy it is to blame your spouse for everything. It is such a convenient thing to do because it means you don't have to take any responsibility. And I'm not saying you have to say you are to blame for everything because you are both at fault in your own ways. But you will get this difficult dialogue on the right foot only by using as neutral language as you can when you answer the question.

If you are having trouble, draw out a timeline on a piece of paper, starting with the date of your relationship started, when you were engaged, when you were married, and so on. Label it with disagreements that come up throughout these times.

It will also be eye-opening to consider how you resolved problems in the past. When you had a big fight about your spouse's parents asking for money five years ago, what did you do to resolve it.

You may have to admit to yourselves that you didn't really solve the problem, and that's OK. At least you are being honest about it now. And now, you can look back at this time and try to learn from it, whether you did the right thing or not.

Everyone knows that relationships get harder the longer you are in them; however, so the disagreement you have now will be your greatest challenge yet. With as little emotion as possible, both of you should brainstorm what you each personally believe is the largest cause of your disagreements.

This deeper question will continue to come up throughout the rest of the workbook, so don't feel pressured to figure it all out right now. You have plenty of time to get closer and closer to an answer.

For now, when you try to answer it, make your main focus your objectivity. Think about the example I gave earlier: should you say the problems started because your spouse's attitude changed, or because they lost their job?

That approach will continue to be important as you go on. Concentrate not on your spouse's flaws, but on external circumstances that can make it hard to be our best selves.

What Do I Do That Gets Under Your Skin?

Anyone in a relationship that has lasted for a decent length of time can answer this question for themselves. But in dialectical behavior therapy, the goal is to express your frustration in a constructive way. As you know, the key to doing that is focusing on one topic at a time.

Try your best not to look at this activity in an accusatory manner, just like with all the others. The main way you will do this effectively is by analyzing your own behavior rather than your spouse's. I do not want you to use this question as an opportunity to bash each other; you will have an opportunity later to ask each other this question.

But for now, ask yourself what you think your spouse will say. Go to a new page in your communication and try to answer this question, trying your best to think about it from your spouse's point of view.

Only after predicting what you think they will say should you two start the next part of the activity. The goal of the first part was to prepare you for whatever they will say. Even if you do get upset by how they describe your annoying habits, you will be better mentally prepared for it now.

Alas, it will not be enough. You will both have to work very hard to preserve the other's feelings as you tell each other what the other does that bothers you. Employ so the tips we have gone over so far, including using "I" statements instead of you-statements.

For instance, you say, "I worry about you when you drink every night" instead of "You're always drinking." You distance the problem a bit from your spouse by doing this. You might want to really drive the point home that you wish they did more, but even so, you shouldn't word it as severely as the second sentence.

But you aren't yet ready to tell each other what habits bother you, because there is one more step you have to take before you do that. Before your partner tells you which of your habits get under their skin, tell them what you wrote down. Tell them what you thought they would say.

Notice that I didn't ask you to write down what they do that bothers you. It simply isn't necessary because you already know what they do that bothers you. You will easily be able to say what your spouse does that bothers you without even thinking about it.

It's considering your partner's feelings and what they will say about you that is hard. It takes thought it isn't something that we even want to do, because we like to see ourselves as blameless.

Ask your spouse the question at the top of this chapter only after you have (1) written in your communication journal what you think they will say and (2) told them what you wrote.

Both when you tell them what you wrote and when you tell them their habits that get under your skin, keep as neutral a tone as possible. Leave your feelings out of it and simply tell them the answer to the question.

Do not mistake being totally neutral from holding back a full answer to the question. Of course, leave out anything petty, but do not leave out any of the habits of your spouse that have a real emotional impact on you. There is a way to do this without making them feel like you are accusing them; for one thing, imagine you were in their shoes listening to your name off their imperfections.

Much in the same way as "I" statements, pay close attention to where the focus is whenever you speak. If you want it to go over smoothly, make the focus on how their habits affect you, not how selfish or lazy they are for doing these things. This framing will be much more effective in getting your spouse to listen to you, and ultimately to change their behavior.

Lastly, I want us to move into the subject of nonverbal communication, which has been a long time coming. It's important that we talk about it because you have to show your partner with more than just your words that you mean well. You have to show with more than just your words that you still love your spouse even as you voice your frustrations, worries, and concerns.

It is a rich topic, but we will do a quick summary that will tell you everything you will need to know to make productive communication with your spouse possible.

The easiest area of nonverbal communication to cover is eye contact. Now, it isn't like you are too shy to make eye contact with your other half, so that isn't something we need to worry about. For the context of a relationship, eye contact mainly serves the purpose of showing your spouse you are listening.

When anyone sees you looking in their eyes, they feel like you are actually paying attention to what they are saying. Much of the conflict in relationships stems from feeling like we are not being listened to, so good eye contact when your spouse is talking will help tremendously to prevent this conflict from arising in the first place.

When your spouse tells you what they guess, you will say their bad habits are, and when they tell you your bad habits, make eye contact with them. They will be convinced that you are really listening to them.

Next, we have body language, which is the broadest topic of all of these. However, in the context of dialectical behavior therapy, there is really only one concept you need to know about body language. It is the concept of congruence.

Broadly, congruence refers to things matching or being the same. If you didn't know it already, it will help you remember this body language concept. In body language, if you have congruence, it means your body language matches with their idea of what you are thinking.

Let me give you an example. You are talking to your significant other about the taxes you are filing this year. You don't want to give them the impression that you are worried about making the tax payments you owe, so you display body language to communicate the idea that you are not worried. You puff out your chest and make a conscious effort not to stutter or shake.

But your spouse can see through it. We don't quite understand how it works, but we all can tell when something is off, and someone is trying to act differently than how they really feel. We can all tell when our spouse is incongruent.

The lesson is not to try to fool each other with misleading body language. Not only will they figure out that you are incongruent, and it won't work, but you are giving them the impression that you don't trust them enough to tell them how you really feel. This is not conducive to fostering trust with your spouse.

When you tell your spouse what habits of theirs get under your skin, don't try to use false body language. Be who you are without editing yourself to be more like you think you are supposed to look.

There are two more areas of nonverbal communication, and they are closely linked: voice and emotion.

You express emotion in a number of different ways without even trying to. You make facial expressions, change the tone of your voice, and have habits like shaking or clenching your jaw.

All of these are cues in nonverbal communication that people can use to read how you are feeling whether you like it or not. Your spouse can read these on you best of all because they know you.

The idea of congruence applies to emotion just as it does to body language. You might think you can display one emotion on the outside and another on the inside without anyone finding out — you are misguided. You are better off being open and authentic with your emotions and dealing with them as they come up.

It is certain that your spouse will tell you things during this activity that will offend you, but it won't help to suppress how you feel during this time. If you hold it down, it will only come out later much stronger.

Even though it is inconvenient, you will have to deal with your emotions as they come up just as with everything in this book.

Finally, there is a tone of voice. But here, we are mainly interested in how our tone of voice can change because of our emotions. While I did say to let your emotions come out during this activity, when it comes to your tone of voice, you are better off trying not to let it affect how your voice sounds.

It is very common for people not to realize how their tone of voice is affecting their message. You may unintentionally offend or hurt your spouse if you don't watch out for this.

Luckily, there is a way you can practice controlling your tone of voice on your own. You have a voice recording app on your phone. Simply speak into it and say sentences with various different emotional tones.

Then listen to them and hear what you personally do differently with your voice to express all these emotions. It will help you not let these emotions slip out on accident when you have this conversation with your spouse.

With everything that you have learned so far, you have everything you need to get through this particular activity. If you two still have issues getting through this part, it might be because you need to return to the more basic questions preceding this one. After spending sufficient time with them, return here and see if there is any improvement.

Why Do You Love Me? Why Do I Love You?

Think about your answer to the question, "How do you relate to each other?" That answer was probably a list of concrete things that got you to find yourself in love with your spouse.

I asked you to consider all the ways you relate to your partner with all the everyday things that make your life together work. Things, like doing the dishes, mowing the lawn, going to work every day, and eating dinner together, can start to feel like ordinary and mundane, but when you step back and think about it, you start to appreciate how all of these things are part of how you relate to each other.

But we know that you don't love someone because of specific habits or personality traits. We love them because we feel they are close to us in a mental and emotional way.

This question asks you to get past the shared interests, friend circles, and such and ask yourselves why you love each other instead of just being friends.

One way to start out is by confronting that question. Why aren't you just friends? It's a helpful question because sometimes it can be quite convincing to make off a list of things that make us stay with our significant other, and the only way we can really challenge that is by pointing out that this list could just be reasons why you are friends.

By the same token, you might have a list of reasons why you are friends with someone, and one might ask why you aren't more than friends. Clearly, there is a reason you are in a romantic and sexual relationship together to the point where you got married. But narrowing down the reason why you built this life together can be rather challenging.

You might be tempted not to answer this question at all. You might think that love can't be quantified or explained. You might be fine with leaving it at that and not answering the question at all.

There are two big reasons you need to get to the bottom of this question, though, whether you like it or not. The first reason is situational, but the other always applies, no matter what kind of marriage this is.

The situational reason is that some people are just the types who need things to be put into words. Sure, there may be one person in the couple who is fine with not defining the reason for their love, but then their other half might still need them to articulate their love in words.

Since you two are the kind of people who read a book to work through their relationship together, it is almost certain you are among these kinds of people.

If both halves of a couple don't need to put it into words, then they won't have this problem. That's why I said it was a situational reason to put your love into words. But even then, you will still need to do it for the next reason.

The next reason is simple, and it will always apply: if you are going to communicate clearly, you are going to have to use words.

Sure, understanding nonverbal communication is still important. But you may have noticed that it is not nearly enough in the messages it sends to communicate clearly. That's what we have words for.

Maybe you want to say that your love is beyond words, but it isn't. The real problem is it takes work for you to find the right words. But when we take the time to find the right words, it is very much worth it.

Notice how the question works with the assumption that you both still love each other— as it should. A couple who didn't love each other wouldn't try to cooperate with this workbook and try to figure out what was wrong. They would have resigned to the fact that the relationship wasn't working anymore a long time ago.

You two didn't do that, and it proves that you still love each other.

Even more importantly, you both are showing that you are willing to put in the work that a relationship requires because you are going through the often difficult process that this can be.

This leaves us with the deeper question of why you love each other. As usual, you first will have to ask yourselves how you feel when you are in a safe, private environment. You can't do it when your spouse is around; if the two of you are together right now going through these questions, this one will be a homework assignment of sorts.

It's not the kind of question you can answer on the spot and get the result you need. Surely you will be able to come up with an answer, but we don't want just any answer. We want the real answer, and you're not likely to get that real and true answer when you are in the presence of your spouse.

You want to know what you really think on the deepest level. It takes time. It takes reflection. It takes being alone. Rather than trying to answer the question, "Why do I love my spouse?" when they are right next to you, give yourself the time and space to answer this properly. It is the only way to get to the accurate answer you need.

If it helps you, please write in your communication journal to try to answer this question. But that's not the assignment I'm giving you, because, in reality, it is more likely that trying to get this answer on paper will get you further from the answer because you will constantly feel like you are leaving something out. With a question as deep as why you love someone, this is common.

You may not think so intuitively, but one of the best things you can do to get to the answer is by enjoying fiction.

That's because fiction helps us let go of the immersion we have in our own life. Strangely, when we get so caught up in the drama of daily life, it's almost like we get immersed in our own life like it is a TV drama — and it's not a good thing, because it makes being objective a complete impossibility.

You lose yourself in all the things you do; you feel like you are becoming part of your environment rather than a living, thinking person who can make their own decisions. Thinking critically about the reasons we love someone is hard in an environment like this.

Any fiction will do, but I recommend written fiction because it is more interactive than any other medium. With text as your only way to create fictional characters and settings, we have to work a lot harder to make the story happen, making it much more immersive than any other medium. But as I said, any medium of fictional storytelling will do.

As a side note, fiction also helps us be more empathetic of other people, including our spouse. Reading or watching fiction will help you be more understanding and kind to them, which will only be good for helping you communicate with them more productively.

You may also find that the words of fictional characters can articulate your own thoughts perfectly. You may not be a romance reader, but you would be surprised at how well those books can put our reasons for love into words. Reading a romance may directly help you find the answer to this question.

Once you are away from the fiction for a bit, the immersion will start to dwindle, and you will be back to thinking about your real life, except you will find that you will feel more clear-headed about this relationship than before. You may have been inspired by the story you lost yourself in. This is one solid strategy for understanding why you love someone.

But as with many things in life, some of it is just waiting for time to pass. You might not know the answer right away, but you will if you wait long enough and have some patience, it will come to you.

When your spouse tells you the reason, they love you, especially if they put as much thought into it as you did for yours, you will feel incredibly affirmed. You will also have a better idea of what you are trying to keep when you work on your relationship. With that said, telling each other your answers to this question will lead you naturally to the next: How do we work together?

How Do We Work Together?

It might seem impossible to work together at this specific point in time, but you can start answering this question by remembering when you last worked together.

Look at the timeline you made and recall the ways you worked together to resolve problems. That should tell you what you should do now.

The ways you worked together need not be deep. For instance, it could be as simple as the time you two worked on a garden together. It could be the way you each do your part for Thanksgiving every year.

It will you figure out how you can work together on some of the specific problems in your relationship.

When you worked together for Thanksgiving, who did what? What problems did you run into while you did this task together, and how did it turn out? What did you two do to make things work out the way they did, for better or for worse?

From here, expand to more everyday ways you already work together without even thinking about it as working together. That includes chores, financial planning, and the like. As you found out in the "How do we relate to each other?" question, we don't always work together in ways that we acknowledge in marriage, because all the things we do together are so intertwined into our daily lives that it just feels normal. But the more you reflect, the more in touch you will be with how you are already working together.

The problem is, when we are working with our partner on more challenging tasks, we are more aware of the fact that we have to work together. If we aren't aware of that, we will make a lot of mistakes.

We like to think that in a previous life, we've been very good at showing our partner how to do something even though in this one, we have to do a lot of things in a row that we aren't very good at. Sometimes we know what we are doing, but other times we don't. It is the problems that we do not see coming that make it harder to work together in a productive way.

We want our significant other to admit to their crimes — and part of starting again is admitting fault and apologizing. We may want to think that we couldn't have done anything wrong. As we've been trying to be more aware of throughout the book, though, none of us are perfect, neither you nor your spouse.

You won't abruptly become more perfect because you are pretending to be. All you are doing is being dishonest with yourself in a way that is extremely counterproductive to working through your issues together. You are better off being yourself in all of your flaws, so you can both at least be open about your flaws and work with them.

Now that you have thought of a time that you two worked together for Thanksgiving and times you work together every day; the next exercise will be about practicing working together right now.

It may be an exceedingly simple task, but it will test how well the two of you can work together so you can (1) get the task done and (2) do it without bickering too much.

Together, find a new meal that you can eat tomorrow. The catch is that it does have to be new, so you can't just say you'll make one of the dishes you cook all the time and be done with it. You need to find a new recipe in a cookbook or somewhere else and then make a plan to get all the ingredients, determine who will do what, and come to an agreement about all of this.

As an extra challenge, I want the two of you to try to get this done in just fifteen minutes. Start a timer as soon as you can, and then get started. When you are done, come back to the workbook so you can have a discussion.

Read on only after you have already done the exercise. Then, ask yourselves some quick questions. What went wrong? What went right?

You should also ask yourselves if you met the two requirements, which were to get the task done and to do it amicably.

Start off by each telling the other what you did right. You want this to be a positive exchange before a negative one. They want to hear good things from you first, and that's a principle that you should apply throughout these exercises: whenever possible, try to let the positive come before the negative.

Only after you cover the positive should you move on to what could improve. Take note of how I didn't say what went wrong, but what could improve. This way, even the negative things sound more positive. It may not seem like it would make a big difference, but it really does, because negative and positive attitudes are contagious.

When you and your spouse learn that you can each work through your disputes without it being filled with negative emotions, you will stop dreading it so much, and you'll get excited to work through things together because you'll know that it doesn't have to be so bad.

It might sound like this couldn't possibly be the case right now, but if you give the methods outlined in this workbook a real shot, you'll see that they really work. It's just that you need to be able to imagine how things could be different.

Sometimes, we lose sight of why we even try to work with our spouse. We may even have thoughts like it isn't worth the pain to work with someone else.

But remember that everything in life comes with benefits and drawbacks. It might sound like it would be better to be alone, and it might seem like everything would be easier. Of course, in some respects, everything would be easier just for not having to work with someone else anymore. But there is more to it than that.

When we have the opportunity to have a spouse who will be there for times that would be difficult alone, we shouldn't take that for granted.

No one can deny that sharing and working with other people can be harder than doing things on our own sometimes. When we get frustrated working through the same problems every day with our spouse, we can't help but think that we would be able to handle it better alone.

Try this. We have issues that we don't think are serious, but affect every aspect of our relationship. What do we think is important to us in our relationship? What do we believe is critical in creating a strong marriage?

But how can we achieve this understanding of what really matters to each of us? By taking the same observations that we used, to begin with. The same questions that we asked before. To turn on the kind of self-talk that will improve our relationship, we must see ourselves through the eyes of our spouse.

But the truth is, you don't even appreciate all the things that are having someone there for you helps with, not the least of which being sheer emotional support. On the surface, it may seem like a small thing, but having someone there for you feels much different from when you are going through hard life experiences such as job loss, the passing of someone we love, and so on all by ourselves.

We don't even think to appreciate having our spouse there when these things happen, because, by their very nature, these things are still so rough to go through.

But try to remember that it would be harder without them there. Try to remember that the most important thing they do for you is just being there. Do all you can to be there for them, too.

What Makes Marriage Work?

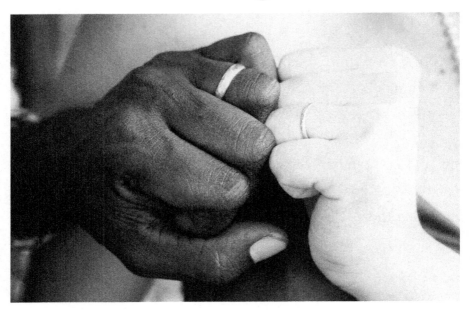

You know other married couples. Now, every marriage has its problems. A healthy, conscious couple will still say things they regret to each other. They will have many of the same problems you do.

The difference is that a healthy, conscious couple approaches each disagreement one at a time and comes to a plan of action after a conversation in which both parties feel heard.

To let this happen in your relationship involves setting healthy boundaries and acknowledging and then discussing your differences and disagreements openly. Having a good time together doesn't have to be a chore. It just has to be what you have time to give each other.

Becoming more like this couple is only a matter of emulating this strategy.

So, let's break down all the things this conscious marriage gets right. There are two main parts to this couple's success: problem-solving and communication. Since it always has to come first, we will go into communication first.

So far, in the workbook, you have learned a ton of communication skills and concepts that will be helpful to you as you try to express more effectively with your partner. Now, dialectical behavior therapy works the same basic way for both communication and problem-solving: we deal with one issue at a time.

We don't allow ourselves to do any more than that, because otherwise we will be overwhelmed, and we might as well not communicate at all if we aren't doing it well.

One issue at a time also means each spouse takes turns speaking. When one spouse is talking, the other does not interrupt. All they do is listen. You can nod your head and make eye contact with them to show them that you are really listening to them and not just waiting until your turn to talk.

Before I delve into some other key points in good communication between a married couple, I would like the two of you to have a discussion about what you think it looks like when a married couple can communicate well. You can think back to a couple you know who does this effectively, although that might be hard to do because couples don't tend to have these difficult conversations around other people.

Thankfully, you probably have at least some examples of times when the two of you managed to communicate well in a difficult situation. Maybe not everything went perfectly. But you can look back on this example and ask yourselves what went right in that particular instance. You can use it as an example for yourselves for the future so you can communicate more like you did that time.

The other main way you can practice good communication for a relationship is by trying to use "I" statements and by working on all four forms of non-verbal communication: eye contact, body language, emotion, and voice. The more aware you are of all of these, the better you will be at tapping into what makes your spouse tick without upsetting them.

Now that you have made a real dent in the workbook, you already have a lot to go off of for what will help you communicate better. As long as you have been doing all the exercises along the way, you are even getting integral practice for improving your relationship communication skills.

Next, there is the other side of what makes a marriage work, and that is problem-solving. You can problem-solve already with your spouse, or else you wouldn't be together right now. However, all of us could improve our problem-solving skills, both inside and outside of our relationships.

As you did for the communication part, I would like to ask both of you to take a moment to discuss what makes for good problem-solving skills. Think back to all the scenarios and ideas we have already gone through to help get your thoughts flowing. Whatever you come up with, coming up with ideas together will be a fruitful way for you to hone practical communication skills.

The two of you should now think of a time when there was a difficult problem, and you worked it out together. As you have probably realized by now, the problem-solving and communication are both highly related things, and so they can be hard to separate. But still, you should try to think of a time when the problem was difficult, specifically, not just when you were able to communicate well.

Financial problems can be great for finding this kind of example. When we go through rough patches with money and have to find places to cut corners, we have to be inventive sometimes and figure out what we will do differently to make sure we are paying our bills.

The answer to problem-solving is always to work through one thing at a time, even when it is tempting to work on many things at once. When confronted with so many problems, we want to force them all to work out at once, but life doesn't work that way. Do your best to have just one problem on your mind that you want to work through, and the rest will follow from there.

Another major part of problem-solving is being humble enough to seek out outside help when you need it. If you are too proud to say to an expert that you need help, you are just dragging out your difficulties much longer than they need to drag out.

Men, in particular, tend to have a problem with asking for outside help. They want to have the appearance of always having things all put together, so they can't risk that facade by showing they can't do everything alone by asking for help.

But on the contrary, if you know you are a man who does this, seeking outside help will only make you seem more reasonable. It shows that you care more about figuring out the problem than preserving your own pride.

When it comes to problem-solving, you have to know when to keep working through something, and when to walk away.

Working hard is a virtue, but hurting yourself by straining yourself on a difficult task isn't always the answer. We can't always solve things with sheer force.

But we can build habits of motivation so that when a seemingly impossible task becomes obvious, we set our sights on something better. I'm not saying we have to be perfect.

Every once in a while, we need to give ourselves a break and approach a new challenge with a positive attitude. Sometimes, our best option is to walk away from it for a while and come back later.

Finally, know that what makes marriage work is the effective combination of both things: productive communication and good problem-solving. A couple who has both of these things will still have hard times like everyone does, but the difference is, they will feel equipped to deal with that when it happens. You and your spouse gain the potential to get there if you both put in the work.

What Is a Communication Skill?

The book so far has equipped you with communication skills to aid in the healing of your marriage. We want you to ask yourselves what you think communication skills are.

I hope the two of you bring up "I" statements, non-verbal communication, and dialectical behavior therapy. As you know, this route of therapy in psychology has a number of attributes, but the main one is the idea of confronting one issue at a time instead of being overwhelmed by all of the potential issues that could come up. With these three communication skills under your belt, you will be well-prepared for dealing with any problems in communication that may come your way.

I want to add in another communication skill that you should add to your list of skills in communication that you need to learn, and that is active listening.

I mentioned it before in the book, but it is worth mentioning again as a skill you should pay special attention to. You can get so much more out of communication with your spouse when you are an active listener. It means you don't just make them believe you are listening so they will listen to you better, but you actually do listen to them.

This sincerely benefits you in the end, since it helps you gain valuable information. It tells you what is on their mind, which can only help you in your relationship. Maybe you don't always make as much effort as you should to get into your significant other's mind, but it is truly worth the small hassle.

You are sure to have noticed examples of effective communication between couples in your daily life. Discuss healthy, conscious couples you know and find conflict resolution strategies that you both like.

Before, you did a similar activity, but it was in the context of what makes a marriage work. This time, I want your focus to be on only the role of communication in a conscious married relationship. Not only that, but I want you to ask yourselves what specific communication skills you think will be the most helpful to you in your specific problems.

For example, if one or both of you are always saying you aren't listened to, both of you should put some effort into honing your active listening. I say both of you should do it because this is how any self-improvement you make in dialectical behavior therapy should be. You may have an idea of who is mostly responsible in your head, but both of you should do it anyway.

For one thing, when both spouses do the same self-improvement practices, we sidestep the problem of blame that we are always trying to avoid in this kind of therapy. For another, you will still get value out of it even if you don't think you need it. People who are better at active listening than your average person can still improve; people who can control the tone of their voice very well can still learn how to do it better.

This is an important thing to do because while this book can give you tools to tackle any situation in your marriage, applying these tools to your real life will be more practical if you can see them in action.

And that is the real purpose of this chapter. So far, you have gotten relatively deep into communication topics, and you have done some of the exercises in the workbook, but most of your exposure to the communication skills had been entirely theoretical. Now, you should take the chance to fix that by doing practice for each of the communication skills we have covered.

For active listening, you and your spouse can listen to the radio or podcasts together. The catch is, one of you should quiz the other on little pieces of information they heard in the program to make sure they are really listening.

To practice controlling the emotional expression we make as part of nonverbal communication. We can look in a mirror with different facial expressions, imagining the emotions that go with them. Next, we can get these same emotions into our imaginations, but without showing them on our faces.

This powerful skill is called state control, and it is tremendously useful to prevent people from getting upset with the emotions they read on our faces.

State control is not taught nearly enough as a communication tool in therapy for couples, but it is an essential component of dialectical behavioral therapy. The reason for this is a simple misunderstanding. People think it is a means of washing all our emotions away and presenting a blank slate, but this isn't the case at all.

The more accurate way to understand state control is to look back on the days when you were a toddler. Back then, you didn't know any level of state control. No one did at that age. When you didn't get your way, you cried until you did. When you felt like crying or screaming, you just did it. You didn't let anyone stop you.

Everyone stops this childish lack of emotional control when they start adulthood at the least, which means everyone has some level of state control. The only difference is how much state control they have. There are a surprising number of people who can't seem to control any of the non-verbal signals that tell others what emotions they are feeling.

We may all have to learn a certain baseline of state control to be able to live in society, but that doesn't mean we're all equally good at it. Some people cannot seem to control themselves even into adulthood, and others seem as though they aren't affected by emotions at all.

All state control comes down to improving the control of the emotions you already have. Whether you have a lot or very little control of your emotions, you can make your emotions become less and less a part of your external presentation if you work at it.

Remember that state control doesn't mean not feeling how you feel. It means not showing it all to everyone. You already know how to do this somewhat from growing up; all you have to do is get even better at it.

All of the communication skills covered thus far can be practiced and reviewed. You and your spouse can practice them together to show each other you are serious about working through your fights.

Is It Worth It to Try to Mend This Relationship?

You will hope the answer is yes, but you need to be honest with your partner and yourself. Do you feel so hurt by your partner that no forgiveness could reverse the psychic damage you endured? Or are you able to see the disagreement as the result of a series of situational factors that can be mitigated in the future? You can always tell which is which by following your gut.

Remember, relationships aren't about the wedding vows— they are about what people do in the present. Those vows can still mean something to you, but it matters so much more what you actually follow through with.

It's not just about following through, either. You can choose to forgive your spouse when they don't live up to your vows, but they say they want to learn from it and do better next time. If you truly love your spouse, forgive him or her.

If you're not willing to address the issues — and find ways to communicate better — then you are in a relationship that is worth sticking with, because you are in a marriage where there are two people who want to make it work.

Relationships start with the passion of affection, but they need to transform into something a little deeper if they are going to last. From what you have learned in the workbook, now that you know all the different communication and problem-solving skills that need to be present in both partners for a conscious, happy marriage, it is easy to see why some people think they would be better off alone.

Passion is powerful, and it is important. In no way do I intend to discount passion as if there is no meaning to it. On some emotional, natural level, you can have a very deep connection with someone that can't be easily put into words. There is certainly value to it.

It is not everything, however. Passion may be the source of life, but it is not the source of all the other things that make a life worth living.

Passion needs boundaries. A marriage worth saving is one in which both spouses understand the limitations of passion in saving their marriage. It can do a lot for them, but it won't take a relationship that doesn't work — because both spouses lack problem-solving and communication skills — and cause it to work.

The real answer to this question lies in the amount of work and effort that both of you were able to put in thus far in the workbook. If you got this far, it is probable that you are in a relationship worth saving, because non-functioning couples would have given up long ago.

There isn't something about the individuals in a couple that makes a marriage work. It's the actions of those individuals and how far they are willing to go so they can stay with their spouse. You can feel; however, you feel about the person you love, but the real display of love is how much you are willing to work for them.

Then it is up to you to reconcile yourself with your partner. They may believe they have messed up too much for there to be any chance of redemption in the future, so it is possible that letting them know you are giving them another chance is completely on you.

On the other hand, maybe you're the one who a long way after messing up. If that's the case, don't push it too much with your spouse. At the end of the day, they are the ones who will have to let you back in. But make it clear that you are willing to keep laboring for your marriage if they will let you.

Where Are We Headed as Individuals?

When someone tells you what they want to do with their lives, this is one aspect of where we are headed: our personal goals. This question wants you to consider things beyond your goals, however.

After all, we can't always choose exactly what happens in life. The only thing you can do for sure is envision what you want to happen beforehand. It may not work out exactly as you want it to, but the practice on its own helps make it more likely. If you can't even imagine something happening, then it definitely isn't possible.

One of the best descriptions of personal goals is "the ladders that guide your travel." Our daily life — the path we're on, the paths we're choosing, and the destinations we're choosing — is the path in which we define our goals, and they define us. And these paths don't change with the season. They don't change with our personalities, with our dreams, with our world experiences, or with the phase of our life when we're working to improve our lives.

We often know where we want to go, and the fact that we don't get to choose it exactly doesn't mean you shouldn't have goals. Now that you have already figured out what your goals are, take some time to determine what unexpected events might come up later in your life.

Start with your financial life and work from there. Do you think you'll be living in the same place? Will you have the same friends? What do you know about what your families will be doing in five years, and how do you fit into that picture?

At first, don't overthink things. Simply close your eyes and ask yourself what you think life will be like for you in five years. Both you and your partner should do this.

Then ask yourselves some logistical questions: will you have children? What kinds of jobs will you work? When is the next big landmark event in the next five years, such as a child's graduation, the lead of a work contract, and so on?

It doesn't have to be a wholly unpleasant conversation. You can talk with wonder about what might happen in the next five to ten years.

But remember that for this question, you are imagining where you, the individual, will end up in the future. It may be hard to think this way, but you aren't thinking of you and your spouse as a unit, at least for the sake of this hypothetical.

You don't have to imagine that you are no longer together, but you just need to think about your future in terms of yourself instead of in terms of what your spouse is doing with you.

Where Are We Headed as a Couple? Where Will We Be in 5 Years?

This question is highly intertwined with the previous one when you see your spouse as a crucial part of your life. Think past yourself and think about you, your spouse, and your household as a whole.

For the last question, I asked you to hold off on thinking about the two of you as a unit for the extent of the question. I wanted you to think only about yourself and where you might end up.

Don't see this question as totally separate from the last one. Instead, ask yourself how the future you imagined for yourself as an individual fits into this future with your spouse and family.

One of the reasons you hesitated to get a divorce (if the extent of your relationship issues are this serious) was because you envisioned this future together, and it is a very hard thing to let go of. There is no one else you can share this exact future with. Ask yourself if fighting for this future is worth it.

At the same time, don't let the huge life shift that a divorce would become the thing the prevents you from getting it. If a divorce is what you as a couple need, then you should come to an agreement and go through with it.

But it isn't likely that this is the case since you are nearly at the end of our relationship workbook. If you didn't have any hope that your relationship could get better, then you wouldn't have come this far. So you should take this opportunity to figure out what kind of future the two of you imagine for each other.

Start out by telling your spouse what future you imagine them having. Then take turns. Enjoy what they say your future will be like. Next, figure out how both of those individual futures work together to keep a household.

It can be easy to think of ways that your spouse might get in the way of the amazing future you see for yourself, but try to look at it in a more positive light. Having someone to support you no matter what you choose to do is definitely a real benefit, even if they will sometimes get on your nerves.

It shouldn't take a long discussion to figure out what you need to do next. If you want to have a future together, then talk about what that future will be. Don't let yourselves delay it any longer with your hesitations about what might come next.

None of us know what comes next, but we can't ever know. We might as well have someone with us to be there no matter what happens, even if we wish they weren't there sometimes. It's better this way than to leave it all behind, except, of course, in the case of an abusive relationship, but that would be a topic for another book.

When you plan a future with your spouse, this is where things can start to get sappy. And that is OK. Just don't expect this to be the lifeblood of the marriage, because this won't be the thing that lasts.

The thing that lasts will be the commitment you make to each other as you show through your actions. You can show each other why you are there for them every day with all the little things you do. Any time you do something for your spouse, even something very small, you are reminding them that the two of you are in this together.

From now on, you can look beyond just this aspect of it. Not only are they going to be with you, but they will be with you for as long as you imagine a future together.

This is why it is so beneficial for the two of you to envision this future together. As long as you have this same vision in your heads, you both feel like you have something you are striving for when you try to keep your relationship thriving no matter what happens.

You may regret things you say to each other or do or don't do. This is completely normal, even in the healthiest, most conscious relationships. But as long as you both have an idea in our head about where you want your lives to go, you will be able to survive anything that life or your spouse throws at you.

Since you have both put in the work up to this chapter, it means you want to be together, too. Don't underestimate the importance of that. When two people are willing to be together despite all they have been through, that is a powerful thing.

What Do We Want?

This is another question for which you should rely on your intuition. Everyone knows what they want. We leave the question intentionally open-ended, because life is rich and complicated, and there are a great many things we all want.

You might find that you don't necessarily see your spouse as part of any of your biggest dreams anymore. If that is the case, you will want to consider what it would be like living without your spouse, as well.

At the end of the day, there are only two options: staying married or not. Both options come with their benefits and pitfalls. We can use our intuition to contemplate what we want and make the decision of what matters most to us.

We all come up with our own reasons for living the way we do. It's no different for how we come up with reasons to be with the partner we have. We stay with them for more than one reason, and that is certain to be true for you and your partner.

After all the questions you have answered, you could probably write a book about all the reasons you two are together. But you don't have to write that book anymore, because right now you are busy writing the story of your lives.

A marriage with two people who see each other in what they want is a beautiful thing. It may not always feel like it is beautiful, but don't forget that love is a rare and joyful thing that should be celebrated, even at times when it feels ordinary and stale. It is only ordinary and stale as long as you let it be with your paradigm on love.

If your paradigm is that nothing is changing and you are getting bored, then the real issue is that you need some changes. You can still get changes while you are in a relationship, so if you still think you need to consider options outside of your partner at that point, then you might unconsciously be wanting out of the relationship. It takes a lot of self-reflection to figure out what you want, so you can't force a single moment to tell you what your answer is.

Are We Both Willing to Change Our Own Habits?

There is one very common problem that comes from resolving our frustrations with our spouse's habits. When someone denies that the habit is bad at all, it leaves their partner feeling frustrated still while simultaneously cutting off any possibility of resolution.

In dialectic behavior therapy, we must consider our spouse's frustrations as valid if we want to have any hope of resolving the problem. It is another issue of whether you want to be right or loved.

You may believe your habit is acceptable, and even if you completely don't understand why your partner would think otherwise, you need to accept the fact that they are truly upset about it. Your spouse is not "wrong" for feeling the way they do.

Recall our lesson about the importance of subjectivity in communication in a relationship. Everyone thinks they are right. This is a very human thing. We think that our partner is crazy for not agreeing with us, in the same way, we think that all the people who don't share all our views on big issues have to be crazy.

You just have to keep in mind that other people don't all think the same way; they all think they are just as right as you do. So any time you are trying to act like you are better than your spouse for not having the habits they have, try to keep in mind that there are definitely things you do that bother them.

It isn't the habits themselves that are the core issue, although you can both work on those habits. The core issue is learning how to be more tolerant of what your spouse does, even if it annoys you.

They see your habits to be just as annoying as you see theirs. In order to fix this situation, it is not the habits that need to change as much as it is your attitudes. All of us are human, and we all do weird things because we aren't perfect.

It might seem like a strange note to give you near the end of the book, but this is the kind of issue that really challenges marriages. Be forgiving of each other's annoying habits instead of being mad at them for not changing.

How Do We Work Together to Strengthen Our Relationship?

Besides the last question, this second-to-last one depends the most on the quality communication you had with your spouse for every other question. You can't make yourself a better, healthier couple before confronting all the larger issues we previously addressed.

Armed with the emotional understanding you have now, it is up to the two of you to figure out how you will work together. How will you ensure the problems you had the last time you tried to make up won't come up again? What will you do in the future if you run into this disagreement again?

The answer to the first question at least has something you can fall back on. If the two of you find that the same problems come up again — even ones that you thought you worked through in here — you should read back through it and see what insights you can find here.

As much as I believe in the insights written below the dialectical behavior therapy questions, I am actually referring to the insights you get from each other during your discussions.

You see, what's more, important than anything you read in these pages is what you actually say to each other in your conversations. Even the topics of the conversation can go by the wayside as long as you are learning how to have productive, open conversations.

Any relationship problem can be resolved if both people in the couple know how to have this kind of conversation. It is a conversation where both of them are allowed to say whatever they want without having to be afraid.

They don't have to worry anymore because they know the foundations of their marriage are strong enough to work through anything that comes their way.

You can have this kind of conversation in your marriage even if you still don't feel like you've had it up to this point. The workbook was written for people who didn't already know how to do this.

The book starts from the beginning with the most basic ideas of communication, and this kind of open conversation is the natural progression of that.

What Now?

The final question is no longer about what you will do to work together in general. You must both face your vices as well as your strengths and make up your mind on what you will do now in this specific situation.

At first, you don't want to go back to the questions you already answered, unless they really call to you. When you reach this last question, your mind should already be formulating something about what you will do.

When you come to one decision together, bring everything you have learned into it, remembering the mistakes you made before, so you don't make them again. They say maintaining a healthy marriage is a 24/7 job, and it's not just a cliché.

Don't expect everything to be perfect from this point — instead, use the tools you have been given to settle the problem when it comes up next time.

Not everything can be summarized that has been covered in here, but you could say the teachings come down to a few things: (1) the idea of dialectical behavior therapy, that is, teaching couples how to focus on one issue at a time instead of having wandering conversations that don't stick to any one issue or resolve anything, (2) productive communication, which is all of the ideas of voicing your ideas while also being receptive to ideas your spouse tells you, (3) problem-solving, the skills revolving around looking at the issue for what it is and making attempts to fix it.

There is much more than this, but if you feel overwhelmed after going through it all and you needed something to sum it all up to make it easier to re-read, this would be a decent way to compile it all into a few bullet points.

It is both of your choices what you want to do from here. You might think you have gotten everything you need out of this book, and you just want to put it away for a while and see how you do without it. It will still be here for you if you should ever need it.

If there was one final note I wanted to give you, it's that both of you should get into the practice of trying to look at your relationship from an outside perspective. You'll never be able to do it perfectly, but the mere attempt will get you to see things more clearly.

Conclusion

Thank you for making it through to the end of *Communication Workbook for Couples*, let's hope it was informative and able to provide you with all of the tools you need to achieve your goals whatever they may be.

Remember that this is a workbook — that means just because you made it from the first page to the end, that doesn't mean you are done.

You are bound to have an argument or two in the future, and if you deal with it without the dialectical therapy approach, you are bound to end up in the same place that got you here. Don't make the same mistake again.

Revisit our questions every time you need them, and you will see a big difference in the quality of your relationship.

It can certainly be tiring to deal with the same problems with your spouse again and again. It makes us feel like they are always the ones causing problems.

The first major theme I wanted you to take from the workbook is that you have to deal with one specific problem at a time. The questions are meant to help you do this successfully because they all get to the heart of things.

But there is a second major theme I hope you find after reading through them all: it is impossible to work through issues with your spouse if you assume everything is their fault — that nothing can be yours.

A lot of people in relationships say that they know their spouse can be right, and they can be wrong. Just not in *this* specific scenario. But that's the kind of thinking you need to let go of.

This specific scenario is what you are dealing with right now. Your task in this workbook is to identify one specific problem and address it with the questions included within. Your task is not to tell your spouse what they are doing wrong; that goes entirely against the point.

When neither spouse in a married couple can't see how they play a part in their issues, there is no way anything can be resolved. Both of them will place the blame entirely on the other, and the issue will come up again and again.

To avoid this, dedicate yourself to understanding the two major themes in the workbook: (1) to work through one issue at a time and (2) to focus on what you as an individual could do differently to help solve the problem.

Of course, approaching things this way requires some trust in your partner. You have to trust that they will do their part in working on improving whatever it is they are doing that makes the problem worse.

But this is just what it means to be in a relationship. You can't let yourself think you only have to help your spouse see what they did wrong. Whatever it is, both of you can do something better that will help you get to the bottom of your problems.

Now that you are there for each other, your bond can be further strengthened. Don't see your issues as a stain on your relationship, but as an opportunity for it to grow. Your attitude affects how you fare in getting over the past. Confront your issues with an open mind, and you are sure to make things better.

Finally, if you found this book useful in any way, a review on Amazon is always appreciated!

Printed in Great Britain
by Amazon

74976990R00078